Dedication Page:

To my hero, my mother.
To my mentor, my uncle.
To my support system, my family, friends, for the man
who loves me and most of all...food.

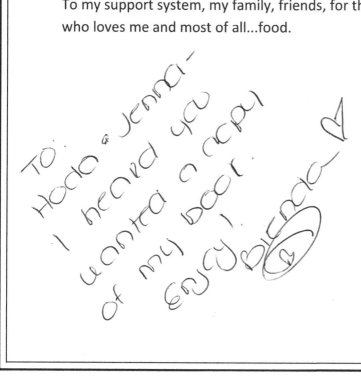

To: Hacto & Jenna -
I heard you
wanted a copy
of my book.
Enjoy! Brenda ♥

Prologue:
Yes, there will be errors.
I ask you to ignore all of that.
Just read, listen, and feel.

Table of Contents

Table of Contents continued

I owe you

What exactly does that mean?
Does it mean you owe me back time?
The time I invested in you.
How about the love that you seem to have for me?
Can you owe that back?
Do I.O.U's ever get paid?
Are they worth even waiting for?
Is the return on investment worth the labor it cost to
obtain?
I owe you,
may be the worst words ever spoken to me.
I have heard those broken promises so many times,
they now mean nothing.
Almost as much as when you say you love me.
Do you?
Do you anymore?
If so, I can't imagine this is how you treat the one you
love.
I would rather you not love me.
I would rather you not owe me.
Because if you do,
pay up now.

Casual

When we met,
it was casual.
You were involved with another.
We went our separate ways.
Was it me?
Or you?

Years later,
we met;
it was casual.
You were married,
I wasn't.
We went our separate ways.
Was it me?
Or you?

Six years later,
we meet again.
You're still married.
I'm not.
You said I wasn't ready.
It is casual?
Or is it not?

Now when we meet,
my heart jumps.
With excitement for more to come.
We go our separate ways.

Is this casual?
Or not?

The next day your back.
You walk through the door.
As we look at one another,
we smile.
And we both know,
it's not casual.

The joke

It was a joke.
Was it?
You can't take a joke?
Can't I?
We can't have fun?
Can't we?
Are we being serious?
Yes.
Aren't we?
Are you serious?
Yes.
Am I?
It was a joke.
I didn't think so.
Are you serious?
Yes.
Why would you do that to me.
Do what?
Disrespect me.
It was a joke.
It was hurtful.
Was it really a joke?
It was.
I can't tell if it was.
You can.
We can't have fun?
Yes,
we can.

I'm serious.
Can't we?
Yes,
we can.

gU̲idance
Never-ending
Conversations
Loss
mEntor

Talks
Independent
Ornery

Mine

I am not going forward.
I cannot handle the responsibility anymore.
Actually, I don't even want to.
I am done with that part of my life.
A simple quiet carefree existence,
that is what I seek.
How to get there,
that is my goal.
I need to figure my path,
my next step.
Plan accordingly.
The next years of my life,
will be my final ones.
I can sense it.
I can definitely feel it.
I want them to be mine.
No ties.
No rules.
No standards.
Except my own.

Cousin Remember?

Our mothers were cousins.
They worked at the umbrella factory.
It was when the boro was the boro.

We had our communion lessons with Delilah's' dad.
He lived on Mechanic Street,
near where our mothers worked.

We had the same babysitter on South Street.
The white house on the corner,
a bodega is next to it now.

Remember the candy store on the corner?
We used to fill a brown paper bag for 5 cents.
We always got the Mary Janes, which stuck to our teeth.

How about the sub shop?
It was across the street from the candy store.
They did have the best subs in town.

You lived on Marcy Street.
A duplex home.
It's still there.

Remember the games we played?
Ring around the rosie, hop scotch, tag,
red light, green light, go!

Remember the clinic?
It was 2 doors down from your house.
We always wondered about the people.

Remember when we were 5 years old?
We ratted on each other for drinking beer.
I can still feel my mother's hand across my face.

Do you remember the sausage casings?
That hung in your mother's kitchen.
I can still envision our mothers as they cooked.

Remember when we wanted to be candy makers?
We collected wrappers from all sorts of sweets.
My favorite candy was the whatchamacallit.

Remember the free bagged lunch we used to get.
It would have a sandwich, apple and carton of milk.
We always carried the lunch bag to the local park.

Remember your mom's restaurant?
It was also on Marcy Street.
I can still see her behind the counter.

Remember the promise we made to each other?
To be one another's godmother, to our first-born child.
This was important to us. Or was it just to me?

Then one day,
you moved away from childish games, talk and dreams.
Your eyes and mind were on other things.

You forgot about me,
our candy making business
and the promise regarding our first-born children.

You weren't even around,
when I broke my hip.
Do you remember?

There was a time,
we were cousins,
dreaming of the future.

Now, we are just two women.
decades later,
miles of distance separating us.

Two adults,
now strangers in the same room,
only joined because two women were cousins.

Mother

This is a difficult month for me.
I tried to ignore what this day stood for.
I went about my day just doing the usual Sunday
hooplah.
Yet, I felt I needed to pay homage to my mother
publicly.
As many others have to theirs.
I was speaking with a friend and she called me an
overachiever.
Yes, I am.
Then I remembered why?
I have a stronger than ox personality,
an overwhelming determination for everything,
a response for everything (yepper),
a strong family unit,
great friends (you know who you are),
a hostess with the most style,
an awesome personality (you know I do)
to list a few things.
I owe all of this to my mother.
I would not be who I am without her.
She formed me into the woman she wanted me to be.

Google defines mother as 'a woman in relation to her
child.'

The bible defines the first mother mentioned, Eve.
Eve means life or living.

Genesis 3:20 says *'the man called his wife's name Eve, because she was the mother of all living.'*

This is my mother,
whomever
or whatever
she came in contact with
came to life.
There are not enough words
to express her zest for life
that was extinguished way too soon.
Many did not have the opportunity to enjoy and love
her.
She is with me in everything I do.
I do it with,
and most of all,
for her.
This is the daughter she raised me to be,
her replica.

What happened

You called at 1am,
this wasn't a booty call.
I hear the hurt in your voice.
I opened the door,
not a word was said.
Something happened.
You always talk.
As you undress and crawl into bed
you pull me close.
I wrap my arms around you.
Breathe my love.
I rub your back.
I try to rub the pain out.
I listen to your erratic breathing
and I rock you in my arms.
Your breathing begins to slow down.
It's going to be ok.
You say nothing.
I hug you tighter.
I rain kisses over your face.
It's ok, your safe.
Don't think my love, just sleep.
You pull me closer.
Your breathing has relaxed.
You take a deep breath
and
tell me
It's over.

I freeze.
What?
How can we be over?
We just started.
Then you go on and speak.
It's over, my marriage is over. I'm done.
I breathe a sigh of relief.
Then say nothing.
You continue to speak.
I listen, absorbing everything.
I still say nothing
You finish speaking.
I rub your hurt.
I rub until my fingers stiffen.
You fall asleep.
You drifted into a deep slumber.
I try to relax my body,
against you,
taking in what just happened.

June 6, 2016

What I love most about my job are the people I meet.
Today I met Louis.
Louis' wife is in skilled nursing.
She is to be transferred to the memory care community.
Louis is a lady's man.
He loves the ladies.
These were his words.
He likes looking, talking and spending time with women.
He stated that he has been with his wife for decades but she now has dementia.
He loved the woman she used to be and they had a wonderful life.
They have 3 great kids.
He became sentimental when he was talking.
Louis talked about being lonely in the house.
He needs a lady around for companionship, cooking, and being intimate with.
He said he had to decide between 2 women.
Both ladies are in their 60's.
He claims he will need to make his decision soon.
He does not want to be alone anymore.
Did I mention that Louis was 95?

The Healing

Now it's time to heal.
I don't know how this goes.
This is new to me.
This took a toll on my person,
my mental capacity.
I wasn't aware of how much,
until it was over.
I'm still not aware of the magnitude of my pain.
The hurt that I have endured.
How does a person
begin to heal.
What do I do?
I don't want to read a book on this.
I just want to be able to feel good again.
Feel me again.
Find myself again.
I lost myself a year ago.
Will it take that long to get back?
Please don't let it be that long.
I don't want to wait.
Do I have to?
I may need to,
to get ME back again.

And the name is

It'll be a few minutes, ok?
I sit and peruse the plethora of colors
- Colors of the rainbow
- Of a cat's eye
- Mermaid
It used to be simple to choose, what you liked.
Pink isn't pink anymore.
There's
- Coral
- Blush
- Bashful
- Seashell
Even black isn't black anymore.
There's
- Midnight
- Metallic
- Matte
There is also a world of names to go with them.
Such as
- I'm feeling sassy
- Bobbing for baubles
- Don't Sweater It
- Office Space

Once again it used to be easy to select a color.
Some names make you turn beet red.
Like

> -Erektis Klitoris
> -Size Matters
> -After Sex
> -Dick Weed
> -Jizz
> -Butt Taco
> -Porn-a-thon
> -Pussy Galore

With so many options who can choose?
I dare you to.
Whatever the name,
let alone shade,
it's worth the look.
Especially, when another asks what color you have on
and you demurely respond with
'Pet my Peacock.'

My frenzy

I am thinking.
Yet, I have no idea
or what thoughts
are passing
through my mind.
Has that ever happened
to anyone else?
I believe I may
be losing it.
I mean,
just the other day
I was looking for my mother's pendant.
I wanted to wear it.
I had this overwhelming
need to locate it
and put it on
at ten o'clock at night.
I could not find it
anywhere.
I know I placed it
somewhere for
safe keeping.
So safe,
I couldn't locate it.

My mind was in overdrive.
Jumping and silently accusing
the absent man in my life.
You robbed me.
You have taken a memento from me.
I am crazed now.
The tears are coming down.
I don't have any clue as to why.
You only came back
to steal
from me.

I am bent over.
My stomach is in knots.
It doesn't matter
that you have thousands
saved in my home.
You have stolen it.
My mother's pendant.
A memory taken away.
A love destroyed.
Pawned away for a mere few dollars.
Then it is at this moment
you call.
I am in the middle of my hysteria.

I stare at the phone,
not wanting to answer.
I lay my head on the pillow.
I want to stay in my irrationality.
Let me stay in my madness.

Where would I be

I cannot recall,
what I was doing before you.
When you are present,
I know what I am doing.
When you are not here,
I seem lost
confused.
When you are here,
I am complete,
whole
wanted
and loved.
In the meantime,
can you not keep me waiting for you?

Things that

Cut

Jackhammer
Nail clipper
A knife
Scissors
A razor
A saw
Hair clippers
Broken glass
Nails/Screws
Axes
Lawn mowers
Pliers
People

Bite

Bugs
Animals
People

Bleed

A paper cut
Your heart
A wound
A thorn
You financially
Your nose
People

Break

- Eggs
- Awkward silence
- Pinatas
- Bad habits
- News story
- World records
- Toys
- Glow sticks
- Chocolate bar
- Zippers
- Ice
- New shoes (breaking them in)
- Homes (breaking into them)
- Gas (pass wind)
- Your car (breaks down)
- Your ego
- Water balloons
- Your heart
- Tree branches
- Furniture/Appliances
- People

Here

I don't know if
I will ever believe,
we are at this place.
A place of comfort.
Formality.
You are
my friend.
my mate.
my equal.
The one that knows me best.
Even what I want for myself.
Each day I see you,
it's all brand new.
Like the first day.
As I sit and look at you,
I see the years etched on your face,
the eyes that are drawn,
the lines imprinted on our skin,
and the hair that is gray.
I hope I wasn't the
cause of any of it.
I look up
and we lock eyes.
We share one breath.

No words are exchanged.
I am glad.
I am here.
To ease the pain,
if I was.

Expecting

It was August 31, 2019 at 12:45pm.
I received the news, it happened.
The tears began to fall.
I drove straight to a friend's home.
For solace, shelter, to collect myself.
After getting myself under control,
I drove to a store.
I walked around mindlessly
before going home and crawling into bed.
The tears quietly fell.
This wasn't 'new' news, this was expected news.
Yet a part of me had hoped it wouldn't happen.
My mind reminisced about our relationship.
I closed my eyes.
I am thankful that you were there for me.
I hoped, I was there for you.
The tears continued to silently fall,
as I recalled your last words to me.
> Our dinners
> Our conversations
There will be no other that can take that role.
Two weeks ago, I saw you last.
I drove 37 hours to see you.
You were worth it.
It was the right time,
for both of us.
Tissue after tissue absorbed the grief.
I still didn't expect it.

I had hoped for anything but this.
When you are expecting,
you still don't expect to hear
the news of your loved one leaving this earth.
You think you're prepared.
That person you knew, was gone, long ago.
The shell of their being is all that was left.
Still, you don't expect it.
When you don't, you aren't prepared.
I tune the world out for the next 5 hours.
I let my grief flow.
When I was done, I raised my head off the pillow.
It didn't feel like a cinder block.
I said a small prayer to my Uncle,
told him to have fun arguing with his sisters.
What you don't expect as you are expecting
is that life goes on.
I expected a miracle,
I didn't receive it.
When you are waiting for the news that you have been
expecting,
know that the world doesn't stop.
I can hear my Uncle now,
        *'Why are you crying? For what? Control yourself
and let that person die in peace.'*
I hope I did that.

Fights

Arguments

Migraines

Irritating

Loyalty

Yelling

Disruption

Coming in late.
Cell phone usage.
Unzipping your bag.
Coughing.
Side bar chatting.
Typing away.
Texting away.
Unwrapping a candy bar.
Opening a beverage.
Sipping a drink.
A pencil begins to tap.
A pen clicks.
Does it end?
No.
Then a snore begins.
I turn my head and look.
Can someone really be sleeping in the middle of all this.
Yes, they can.
A laughter,
or is it a chuckle.
I hear a sigh.
Or was it a groan.
There's a crunch,
like biting into a chip.
A chair squeaks.
Someone's stomach rumbles.
Another laugh or chuckle.
Someone has hit the volume button on their laptop,

that adds to the disruption.
What are these people doing?
More tapping,
typing,
clicking away.
Then the words are finally said,
class dismissed.
The best disruption,
until next time.

I **oscopy** you

Endoscopy
Biopsy
Then a Thyroidectomy.

Endometriosis biopsy
Colposcopy
Then a **Hysteroscopy**.

I feel so **macroscopy**.

Colonoscopy
Cystoscopy
I think I even had **arthroscopy**.

I NEED to find my **centroscopy**.

If someone would attempt a divination of **geloscopy**,
maybe these medical procedures would not be so
damaging.

I feel **microscopy**,
yet viewing everything in a **stereoscopy** form.

Do not confuse this with **mixoscopy**,

where it is related to voyeurism.

Fundoscopy does not MEAN what I thought it did.

Maybe if they performed a **cranioscopy**,
I would have known.

I would prefer **heautoscopy**,
seeing myself from a distance.

Maybe then,
it would not feel like I was just given a **rectoscopy**.

The Last

This will be the last time we see each other.
Will you remember me?
Will memories flash back to you?
Will you remember me,
family,
us?

The time has flown by so quickly.
Tomorrow I will be gone.
Will you miss me?
Will you recall the things we have done together?
Our last laugh?
Our last meal?
Our last talk?
The last place we visited?

I capture it all in a photo.
Our last picture.
Is that enough?
For me?
Will that sustain,
my memory of you.

I don't think I will be returning before you are gone.
When I get the call,
it will be too late.
Is it selfish to say do not leave me?
Then I will be selfish,

do not leave me.
Let another go.
Let someone else take your place.

I am scared.
Scared that you won't recall me.
More scared,
that I will forget you.
Even more terrified,
that I will forget all of our last lasts.

No other

I see you,
you look my way.
I smile,
and boldly look back.
Our eyes lock,
saying much,
but verbally expressing nothing.
You take my hand,
and press a kiss to it.
I glance down.
Silently,
I thank
that you are here.
No other but you,
would I want,
here.

The arrival of C

Non-small cell carcinoma lung cancer
were the words that hung in the air.
No one spoke.
A deafening silence followed.
It seemed like ages as time ticked away
but it was not.
Yet, it does when your world has changed in less than
three seconds.
Those were the words spoken from the emergency
room doctor.
It did not sound good.
When something does not sound positive,
there is a huge possibility
that nothing will ever be the same again.
Everyone stood still as the family looked around for an
answer,
a response,
or guidance on how to proceed.
The doctor seemed offended when a request was made
to recheck his findings.
The professional apologized
and stated that the oncologist would be coming in to
speak with us.
Oncologist,
a familiar title for a different family member
but not for us,
until now.
The oncologist arrived.

He began to speak a foreign medical language that made no sense.
Yet, mom seemed to know,
have a sense,
possibly anticipated this diagnosis.
Every 5-6 months mom was diagnosed with either bronchitis
or
pneumonia
from her many trips to the emergency room.
We expected another misdiagnosis
of bronchitis
or pneumonia.
We did not expect to hear cancer.
Even though mom's only visible symptom was a cough that would not go away,
this should have been the warning sign.
Something was not right.

The Beach

We weren't on the beach,
except the one time.
You quickly turn your head to me.
Did I say something wrong?
Did I confuse you with another?
You ask me a question.
I am trying to go through the archives in my mind.
No, it wasn't you,
it was another.
I don't like the beach.
I don't like the sand between my toes.
You can't believe that, you tell me, I wouldn't have
thought that.
I am still trying to rifle through the rolodex,
of past involvements.
I was only at the beach 3x (two on dates) the other work
related.
I can't recall any other times.
You ponder my response.
I ask your thoughts.
Your unspoken words are telling me,
we have been together.
I don't recall the beach,
at least not with you.

Help

Through the years,

I supported you.

I heard your cries and helped.

I heard your pain and comforted you.

You were lost and I guided you.

You were confused and I assisted you.

Now I need those things,

where are you?

Looking

When I look at you,
my eyes soften.
I think of how we arrived here.
How it seemed like yesterday,
I saw you.
You didn't see me though.
You saw through me.
That was ok,
then.
Because we are here,
now.
You look at me.
Thankfully you look at me,
now.

Hefe

It is time,
already?
It went by so fast.
I do not want to go.
I do not want to drive.
I do not look forward to seeing you.
I had thought I could handle it.
When I see you, I cringe.
Not because of fear.
I do not like to use the word hate.
I will go with a strong dislike.
I cannot even look at you.
Something so easy,
you make hard.
When you speak to me,
I try to tune you out.
I am obligated to listen.
I don't speak,
I barely even listen to your words.
I look at you from my side vision.
If I see you,
I might gouge your eyes out.
Can you go away now?
I will finish what you want.

I still cringe with dislike,
for you.
Stop talking to me.
Do not look at me anymore.
Just don't.
Please just go away!

My relationship with Cal

I needed to face you.
That is when I decided,
that I was not going to let you get to me.
I can and will get through this.
After our second encounter,
I broke down,
called my sister
and poured my frustration out.
I am positive you brought others to tears.
  To confusion, which I let you do to me.
  To frustration, which I allowed you to get to me.
  To quit, which I will not do.
You have won the first round,
by breaking me down emotionally.
I will win the final bout, Cal.

OK Cal,
We keep meeting.
Eventually one of us will toss in the towel.
I refuse to give in.
As I sat and listened, I began to comprehend some of
the information.
You went a bit slower, not like a speed demon this time.
I was able to understand you better.
If you continue at this pace, we will be on the same
page.

I was not scared; I am not freaking out.
I am not complaining?
Is it because I am comfortable with you?
Can that be possible?
We have only met 3x, I am feeling like we are on the same track.
Yet, I do not want to jinx this.
I am still attending my counseling sessions,
to understand our relationship.
I just may have a chance at figuring you out.

Cal,
I was advised on how to handle you.
A week of mentally preparing for our visits.
I reworked everything you gave me.
The confusion of words still puzzling me.
All the work,
I put in this past week,
comes down to tonight.

I am not ready for this.
Why do I have to?
Why am I putting myself through this?
I am NOT ready, I tell you.
No one hears me.
No one listens to my cries
Or are they complaints?
I am not ready but I have to.

I do not think I will be able to follow through with it.
It is time, there's no holding back.
I hesitate walking through the door.
I take a few deep breaths.
I push the door open.
I take my seat, sit and wait.
The time is clicking very fast.
I blink, once, and it is time.
Head-to-head, toe to toe.
I take several gulps of air.
I look down and then I begin.
I blink and it is over.

The time flew by.
I JUST STARTED,
I screamed in my head.
It cannot be over,
I did not have enough time.
I did not understand what was going on.
As I gathered my things and walked out,
all I can think is….
you won this round.

Cal, you got the best of me.
I studied you for hours and failed.
I do not like to fail.
I do not like the feeling of someone
getting the better of me
but
you're getting to me.

And not in a good way.
I am lacking sleep.
Eating too much garbage.
I am stressed.
My anxiety is at an all-time high.
I feel nauseated.
Migraines have even started.
I feel like I'm beginning to get a medical condition.
This nightmare is pushing me to the brink.

I am ready for this to be over.
I voice my concerns to anyone who will hear them.
Complaints that sound like I am whining.
You now have me whining?
When did I begin to whine?
I can't believe you got me to this point.

I am mad.
Why did I listen at all?
Why didn't I follow my instinct?
I wasn't ready for this.
I knew it.
I was persuaded into this.
I should not have followed the advice of others.

Damn Cal,
why am I here with you?
This relationship is toxic to me.
I need this to end.
Will it?

When?
I know it is not soon enough.
Suck it up, I tell myself.
The decision was made.
I am in it deep.

Your winning Cal.
I am doing everything I can,
to not tap out.
To continue, to finish.
I know I won't win.
I met my enemy and it's you.
I have never disliked anything or anyone as much.

THIS means failing.
This is an avenue I am not familiar with.
A feeling of despair.
Hopelessness.
I am dejected.
I feel unsuccessful.
I can't shake this off.
I am an emotional rollercoaster.
Angry that you won,
pissed that I may have failed myself.

I am euphorically happy that it is almost over.
This was a disastrous experience,
but I will return to a bit of normalcy in my life.
THIS relationship is almost over.
I will be able to sleep now.

Spend time with friends and family.
Reinstate by healthy living ways.
Although it was toxic,
I learned a valuable lesson.
DO NOT let anyone make your decisions.
I didn't listen to myself.
I was swayed into this relationship.
I won't make the same mistake again.

As I look back at all of our meetings,
I wrote your every word down.
I have to applaud myself for taking you on.
I may not have won, but I didn't lose without fighting.

The finale has occurred.
Even though I knew what the end result would be,
it was still an emotional drain on me.
I spent all that time with you.
You couldn't be lenient,
less strict,
less harsh or even generous?
Our time together dragged on like a boring sermon.

Well Cal,
it's over.
The stress, anxiety and frustration are done.
I made it.
I lacked sleep, I binged ate, loss time with friends and
family over you.
I am not happy, not even content but

glad that it is all over (for now).
I even celebrated the occasion.
Even though I gave it my all,
I plunged through the difficulty.
I ignored others that encouraged me to quit.
I still moved forward.
Because even if I failed you,
I couldn't fail myself more.

A second time with Cal

We meet again.
I cannot believe,
I am here with you again.
I thought it was over.
I thought we were through.
I am back here again.

Even before I walked into the room,
my anxiety started.
Why am I putting myself through this, again?
Will I learn?
Will you fail me again?
I am so done with this that I barely put any effort.
I should but I don't.
I am past this and want it to be over.
Will it?
Or will we meet a third time?

The End

I cannot believe it.
I did it.
We are done.
The months,
the weeks,
the days,
that it took
are over.
I can breathe a sigh of relief.
The anguish,
the stress,
the anxiety has been lifted.
I did not think this would ever happen.
Our meeting dates
and
times
are no more.

I am still not able to believe it.
I asked several people if it was true,
has it really happened?
I have been told yes; it has.
Accept it.
It really is over.
I can move on.
Even though it cost me more than I expected,
it won't cost me anymore.
That chapter is now closed.

Take care of yourself Cal.
I will not miss you.
I have packed you away
in a far deep corner
with a lock and no key.

D-Day

Today is the day.
I set the alarm.
Is that why I couldn't sleep?
Why I was up at 3:30am.
Was I anxious?
No, who would be?
Maybe fearful?
Yes, I was.
What if I couldn't go through with it?
I've started and stopped so many times?
Will this be the same rollercoaster?
Do I do this to myself again?
And again?
Why do I do this again and again?
I need to.
Nothing changes,
if I don't make this change.
The alarm sounds off,
like a blaring screech.
Exactly what I need to wake me.
I shut it off on the first ring.
Then I don't move.
I lay in bed motionless.
A few seconds more.
Please, that's all I need.
Let me enjoy a few seconds more.
Ok, minutes then.
OK, half an hour has passed.

GET UP,
I yell to myself.
Today IS the day.
I'm up!

Am I dressed properly, yes.
The right footwear, yes.
Do I need anything else?
No.
I leave,
motivating myself.
I take a deep breath, open the door and head
downstairs.
I tell my sister where I'm going.
OK, 10 minutes.
Huh?
It's been months.
Right!

I start,
my heart is pounding,
I think it may jump out of my chest.
My breathing is all over the place.
I can't control it.
I try to take deep even breaths to steady it.
Yet it sounds like gulps of air.
I sound like an overheated race horse.
Does anyone hear me?
Now I'm parched.

There's no place for a drink around here!
Will I be the first person to die of thirst?

Ok,
calm down.
It's not that bad.
Aaaaaacchch!
I feel a sudden discomfort in my side.
My body is screaming in pain.
Are you kidding me!
Will someone see me if I fall over?
Will they help me?
Or will they laugh?
I didn't bring my cell phone.
Will someone at least call 911 for me!
How much longer will I have to endure this?
I pull the sleeve back on my wrist.
I cringe,
to see that my Fitbit
has informed me
that I have only been walking for 3 minutes.

The man who loves me

You reentered my life.
I needed you, but didn't know.
I hear you speak.
I think how lucky I am.
How lucky we are.
Lucky that we are here together.
This is our chance,
possibly the only opportunity for us.
I will take it.
I won't let this slip me by.
I have been waiting for this.
Waiting for us.
How will we be?
What will happen?
You say I am overthinking.
Let it flow.
I can't do that.
I don't want to ruin this,
jeopardize us.
There may not be another possibility.
I can't screw this up.
The anticipation for this to be right,
sends my stomach in a twist.
What are the odds of it not working?

What happens if it does?
You are the only man who has told me
that they love me.
It's not an accident,
or a coincidence.
It's meant to be.

It's over

I woke up one morning and knew I could NOT go on any longer.
I thought about it all weekend long.
I knew this relationship was over.
I could not see myself step through your door anymore.
I did not want to hear your voice another day.
The last 3 years with you,
were toxic,
like poison running through my veins.

I was done with the sleepless nights.
I was done crawling out of bed in the middle of the night for you.
I was done with having to be the only one carrying this load.
I was done with putting the bandages on this relationship.
I was done without having any support from you.
I was done being on call, 24/7 for you.
I was done.

I called to tell you
but you didn't want to see me.
I dedicated 21 years to you.

I exhausted 21 years,
of fixing you.
I devoted 21 years,
dealing with the drama.
After 21 years,
I was walking away.
I gave you 21 years,
and I was not giving you a second more.

I am fine with that

I was in the 4th grade.
I was in gym class.
I heard my name being called.
I stepped on the scale.
The gym teacher said, '*144 lbs.*'
I stepped off the scale.
He shook his head as I walked by.

I waited in line.
I grabbed my lunch.
I heard a whisper.
'*She's 144 lbs.*'
I kept walking.

I met my best friend,
who was my twin in every way.
I asked her if she was weighed today,
she said yes.
I told her what my weight was,
she weighed about the same.
I told her about the girls at lunch.
'*Don't mind them.*'
'*Why are they talking about it?*'
'*You don't know?*'

'Know what?'
She said, 'You're fat.'
Quickly she said 'We're fat.'
'Huh?'
'They're skinny,' as she pointed at the girls.
'We are chubby,' as she pointed to our bodies.
I told her I was fine with that.

I was in the 8th grade.
I was in gym glass.
I heard my name being called.
I stepped on the scale.
I heard the gym teacher say 220 lbs.
I stepped off the scale.
The gym teacher shook her head.
I headed to my next class.
My classmates were standing around talking about their weight.
One girl exclaimed 'I can't believe I weigh 125lbs.'
Another asked me how much I weighed.
I stood there.
I heard a whisper.
I continued standing,
looking at the girls talking about their 125 lb. selves,
and then whispering.
I was 220 lbs. at 14 years old.

I was not fine with that.

I was in high school.
I was in gym class.
I heard my name being called.
I stepped on the scale.
I told the gym teacher not to tell me.
He shook his head,
as I stepped off the scale.

I walked away feeling fat.
This fat was with me through high school,
where aside from carrying the physical weight,
I had the emotional baggage as well.

I was in college.
There was no gym class.
There was no gym teacher.
I was given a reprieve.
There were no stares,
no looks,
no whispers,
and no questions.
There were other fat people.
I was not the only one.
I fit in.

I was fine with that.

I was a college graduate.
I was on my own.
Real life began,
responsibilities,
there was no thought of weight.
At this point in my life,
my plumpness was becoming sexy to others.
I enhanced my attributes and was proud.

I was 45 years old.
The doctor called my name.
I stepped on the scale.
Even though I do not like the number I see,
I am ok with it.
I stepped off the scale.
He writes the number down in his chart.
He looks at me and I wait.
He shakes his head,
and asks me if I have thought about weight loss surgery.
A memory flashes through my mind of friends who have
had the 'surgery.'
Several who are walking skeletons with bags of skin.
Friends, who were healthier before the surgery.
Who now have scars as the price for thinness.

An ex-friend, who commented that she *'didn't know that leather could stretch that far'* when seeing leather pants on a plus size woman.
I tell my doctor, 'No…. *there has to be some fat people left to balance out the world and who love themselves, as is.'*

For 35 years I put myself through almost every diet craze,
starvation method,
extreme weight loss avenue
just to end up being the person I was meant to be
since the 4th grade.

I am a plus size,
full figured,
cute to boot chubby chick.
I am fine with that.

Untitled 1

I waited.
It's what I do.
For me, you are worth it.
I wonder, would you do the same for me?
I think I wait more,
than spend time with you.
There is something that I like,
yet don't know about it all.
While I wait,
I overthink.
You tell me not to
but it's what I do.
I think about us
and when we are together.
I think about how we have this chance, to be one.
Even if these are stolen moments,
there is no other but you.
I know you feel the same.
Your actions tell me when we are together.
They say something else when we are apart.
When you say one thing and do another.
Why?
Do I not matter?

The Fighters

I began to compare the differences between my uncle and my mom.
My uncle who battled in Vietnam and my mom who fought her entire life.
They chose to fight their cancer differently.
My uncle was diagnosed at 70 and retired.
My mother was diagnosed at 55 and worked until the cancer spread.
My uncle heard I was coming to visit and mowed the lawn.
My mom knew I was coming home, her words to me were, '*I waited for you.*'
My uncle refused treatment and surgery.
My mother decided on treatment, until her body and mind gave out.
My uncle waited in his recliner for his day to come.
My mom wanted to see Las Vegas, one last time.
I asked my uncle if there was anything he needed.
He said, '*No. I have done everything. I have been everywhere.*'
My mother began her treatment, we were on borrowed time.
After visiting my uncle, I hugged him.
His final words to me were, '*Kathy will call you.*'
When my mom could go on no longer,

her final words to me were, *'I don't want to leave you alone, unsupported.'*
Nothing was left unsaid between my uncle and I.
My mother passed away, we said everything we needed to say.
I hugged my uncle, the last link to my mom.
I pushed his once dark brown curly hair back.
I rained kisses on his forehead imprinting my mark for him to carry.
He returned my hug and kissed my cheek.
I asked for his blessing.
My uncle choked up (he has never showed emotion.)
As I bow my head, he blessed me and I heard the tears in his voice.
We said what we needed to say to one another.
The words have been spoken;
the actions were completed.
I was content.
Each fighter fighting their battle the way they wanted.
I am thankful I was here,
before their final bell.

Trying

I'm trying.
Those words are hard to acknowledge.
To myself.
To you even.

I'm trying.
But what am I really trying for?
In being someone else,
so, you won't walk away.
Holding my tongue,
for you to think me docile.

I'm trying.
So, you feel wanted.
For me to seem weak.
So, you think you are needed.
I'm trying to not be those things.

Except I am.
I am trying.
Because I care for you.
That is why you are here.
I am weak.
Where you are concerned.

The only man who has cared for me.
I am weak for.
Therefore,
I will continue trying.

My Hero

I was born between my sister and brother.
My sister was 2 years older.
My brother was 9 years younger.
My sister was your best friend.
My brother was the son you always wanted.
My sister was a grade C student.
My brother was just a student.
My sister was a homebody.
My brother was somebody.
My uncle, told me that he feared for my life.
My uncle, your brother,
saw the broom,
     saw the belt,
          saw the frying pan,
               saw the switches,
and saw the LOVE you gave to ME.
The strength I have,
you beat into me.
The passion I have,
you slapped into me.
The fear that I hide, you verbalized to me.
The strength I saw diminish from your body,
is a daily memory.
The passions that I saw leave your eyes, still burn
through me.
You left this earth, I haven't accepted.

Somehow

Four decades ago
I ran up to you
trying to apologize.

You told me
I confused
you with another.

Just yesterday,
I pestered you
and we became the best of friends.

I blinked
and we were having
our graduation photo taken together.

Where did the time go?
I can still feel the rain on my face
as we walked side by side on the school playground.

Or the many road trips
on I95 south
heading to destinations unknown.

I remember you packing the cassette tapes,
making our selection
singing to 80's music as we drove.

Then we came to blows
brought on by others,
who were no longer in our life.

Neither one of us,
knowing why
it even happened.

We had a sistership
then there was a break.
A mourning period occurred.

Somehow, there was a reunion.
We picked up where we left off.
Stronger than before.

Then, another break.
This one hurt, it hurt deep.
This damage lasted for years.

No type of intervention
could help me heal.
I felt it all.

The years flew by.
Then one day,
my car drove to your house.

Somehow
the doorbell rang
and you opened the door.

Neediness

When did I become so needy?
I recall a time when I did what I did,
and didn't look for confirmation.
Was it so long ago?
When did I change?
I know it changed.
I can't describe what has changed about me.
The exterior is still in a plus size form.
My hair is still short.
My eyes are still brown.
I have the same voice.
My foot size hasn't changed.
Did I change inside?
Maybe.
I don't let the drama of others interfere.
I don't have the time for shenanigans.
I am still passionate about my goals.
I can snap in a blink,
when I am pushed or aggravated.
I have changed that.
I love someone now.
Is that when I became needy?
Looking for your approval in all I do?
It can't be.

That's definitely not me.
Why would I do that?
Why would I seek your affirmation?
If I had an answer,
I wouldn't ask.
I need to know.
There's that word again, need.
The one word that defines me now.
Do I need?
Am I needy?
Does need change me for the better?
Isn't need a form of weakness?
I think I need to know.
I don't want to, if it is.
Yet, isn't need what has made me softer.
The need for you.
I think I need to know.

The soundless meeting

I'm early, so I wait.
I am not nervous.
No one speaks to me.
There is an uncomfortable silence in the room.
This is definitely not what I expected.
There's no talking.
All you hear is my pen.
As I write, someone is drinking their water.
The heat is coming on.
This is definitely not what I was expecting.
The silence is deafening.
Wait, someone has coughed.
Finally, there is sound.
Then quickly, it reverts back to stillness.
Someone has shifted in their seat.
A question is asked.
The quietude is resumed.
There are no beverages offered.
No one is partaking in idle chatter.
So unusual.
Someone has walked in.
There's NOW sound.
Thank you

Unknown

I can't explain it.
You are angry.
You tell me you're limited.
I say you are not.
You have complete control over me.
No,
we both know that is not true.
Only in some things.
Don't I trust you.
That's not a question,
I care to answer.
The moisture leaves a trail on my face.
I have no answer for you.
I can't explain it.
I don't know what it is.
If I knew I would tell you.
You begin to leave.
I call you by the pet name I have given you.
The endearment you have answered to, for 3 years.
You look at me and toss it back.
You are more than angry.
There is disgust within you.
I am sensing a loathing towards me.
I cannot look at you
I begin to find something to hide behind
to mask the hurt,
the shame,
the embarrassment.

I am on full display.
Like an exhibition,
an oddity.
I am feeling all of this in mere seconds.
Then you sit by me,
I try to shield myself.
You don't allow me to.
You want to know.
Where are we going with this?
I don't have an answer.
Why are you limiting me?
I still don't respond.
Tell me.
I can't tell you what
I don't know.
I can't tell you what
you want to hear.
I can't explain it.
I'm scared
but I don't know why.
Let yourself go.
I can't.

The Mason

The walls were built up through the years.
A solid foundation it was built on.
One brick at a time was laid.
A brick for lost childhood friends.
Another for being bullied.
A brick for no Valentine's Day cards.
Another for no date to the dance.
A brick for a teacher who questioned my weight.
One for missing curfew.
Another for being punished.
A brick for bringing a 'C' home.
A wagon full of bricks for the beatings I took.
A ton of bricks for the family.
A brick for not walking for almost 2 years.
A cinder block to stretch my leg out.
A brick when I was homeschooled.
A boulder when I was touched.
Another for wishes not coming through.
A brick when I told you I skipped my period.
A brick thrown at me, when you walked away.
One brick when I took a pregnancy test.
Another when I had to take a blood test.
A ton of bricks dropped when you reached out 5
months later.

The wall was built, a strong foundation it was built on.

Then YOU came and took a sledgehammer to the wall.
The bricks began to crumble.
You took another swing, and the wall was demolished
into rubble.
The wall was not drilled into the foundation.
The bricks were not pressed into the mortar.
The bricks were not tied to studs.
The wall can be rebuilt on a stronger foundation,
with the right materials
but not now.

Talk

I was 11 when it happened.
I wasn't prepared.
No one had a talk with me.
The school nurse briefly brought up the topic.

I was 16 when it happened.
He kissed me, I felt something.
No one had a talk with me.
It was taboo in our family to bring up the topic.
All mom said was, don't come home pregnant.

I was 19 when it happened.
I wasn't prepared.
No one had a talk with me.
I found out the hard way.

I was 47 when it happened.
Still, no one had a talk with me.
I found out with *the one*.
He spoke WITH me.

I am 49, it is still happening.
HE continues to speak WITH ME
and show me what I need to know.

The last year

When I made the decision, I was 100% sure.
Now I am 100% not.
I don't know what has changed.
Is it the amount of work?
Is it that I am over it?
Or am I not challenged anymore.
I just don't know.
I've invested so much already.
I don't have much time left.
Yet, I wonder if I can pull through it all.
Finish what I began,
thirty years ago.
I don't want to short myself again.
This is my last chance.
There's no more.
No 3x the charm.
Is this the 100% I need to get back?
What will it take, if not this?
How do I change,
to get back what I wanted a year ago?
Help.
I need an idea.
I don't want to lose,
the last year I have left.

My soul mate

I met my soulmate the day after Christmas.
It was the best present I ever received.
He adored me for me.
He found ME sexy, just the way I was.
He made me feel dainty and very much a lady.
I felt all of the songs that were about relationships and romance I could now relate to.
I was part of that rare clique.
Me.
I was in.
I was happy to find my equal in all of the ways, which made me whole.

I knew he was THE ONE.
He was the one; I could talk to about any topic.
He was the one that I could call my own.
He was the one that I could take pictures with and show others.
He was the one I could hug, without the *'I am not the hugger type'* response.
He was the one I could hold hands with, without hearing *'I don't hold hands.'*
He was the one I could kiss, without hearing the words, *'I am not the kissing type.'*

He was the one I loved.
He was THE ONE.

My soul mate disappeared one day,
and then a day turned into weeks.
What a rush of relief that I was able to locate him.
He was safe.
He was safe,
with his wife.

I was hurt for weeks.
Then I thought of us,
about what WE had,
about what WE shared.
I knew that he was still THE ONE
and I wanted to be with him, regardless.

I was happy with the moments we shared
part time moments.
I was happy with the time we spent with one another
stolen time.

Then one day HER name showed up on his phone.
Of course, yes, she had a name and it was ___
I asked him about my name.

He responded, *'You have no name, you're just a number.'*
My soul mate disappeared after that.
I was just a number.

Support

6 months ago, I was lighter in mind, heart and body.
The stress,
the worry,
the exhaustion has gotten me to fall back on my ways.
My comfortable ways.
What I know doesn't disappoint me.
The knowledge that regardless of anything,
I can turn to you and you don't judge.
No matter the time of day,
you are always there.
I can't explain the connection we have but does it matter?
Knowing you are there to support me is all I need to know.
Some say it's an addiction.
How can it be if you make me feel
     Satisfied
     Lighthearted
     Appeased
     Filled
     Satiated
     Content
     Happy
     Intoxicated
Even if these are temporary,
At this moment, this is what I need from no one but you.
From you,
I will take it.
You don't discriminate.

You don't write me off.
You don't criticize.
You understand this urgency I require.
You quietly give and I am exhilarated to take.
I know I will soon be in a state of peaceful happiness,
once I have placed my order
of the #1 with cheese and a diet coke.

The Birds

I awoke and could see
the sun shining outside.
I opened the windows
to let the winter staleness out
and the fresh air in.
I began my morning routine.
Then I heard birds chirping.
I became excited.
A symbol of early spring.
The sound brought back
fond memories of my mother.
I can envision her in the garden
tending to her yellow roses.
The birds seemed to be communicating,
animated towards one another.
Reminding me of the
days when my friends and I
would sit, chat and laugh.
As if it was yesterday.
The sound of the birds became louder
as if they too were excited by the warm weather
approaching.
A memory flashes in my mind
of running through a meadow of greenery

with my best friend
when we were 12.
The birds continued,
almost sounding like
bells-like a melody.
I recalled my time
in the choir.
There seems to be one bird,
louder than the others.
Maybe excited for the arrival of their mother.
Suddenly the birds stopped.
Then I hear a female voice say,
"Hello? Hello? Are you there?
Darn, they hung up!"

A few...men

Maybe I was 7 or 8, when I was first touched.
It was the neighbor's son.
Richard

I was 11, when my cycle began.
I was excited to be wearing my new jeans that day.
Calvin

My first crush gave me a necklace.
It turned my neck green.
Walter

I was 16. It was my first kiss.
No one told me that he would stick his tongue in my mouth.
Eric

The thief who took my virginity, without my consent.
He wanted to marry me.
Jose Miguel

I was 20, when I met a Frenchman.
I mixed business with pleasure.
Pierre

We were pen pals, a sergeant in the U.S. Army.
He gave me an ultimatum, my family or him.
Ricky N.

The man who I fell hard for.
Even requesting to have a child together.
Jwel

The first man who ever slept overnight, in my bed.
Underneath my parents' roof.
Raymond

The one who disappeared, and then reappeared.
After I skipped my cycle.
Dion

We met, when I asked for directions.
We ended when you wanted me to take a 'happy' pill.
Caesar

The first and only man who has told me he loved me.
It took him 20 years.
D.L.

The man who has been with me since day one.
The one who is always watching my pockets.
Dad

My advisor.
My mentor.
Uncle Luis

The first man who ever sent me flowers.
He was also the same man who ever slapped me.
Paul

The first guy who I went parking with.
He is the same man who got me out of a knife fight.
Leo

The only man who ever called me a 'spic'.
Not affectionately.
Neso

My first male traveling companion.
He carried my luggage in Europe.
Ricky T. (don't confuse him with Ricky N).

The man who first made me a home cooked dinner,
from scratch.
Eric S. (don't confuse him with kissing Eric)

The only man I have ever picked up from jail.
I should have left him there.
Travis

The first man who massaged my feet.
He was also the first man who told me he loved me.
D.L.

The first and only man who rescued me,
when my car broke down.
Dad

The first man who kissed me passionately,
is same man who gave me a full body massage.
D.L.

Through the years the fillers, who entertained me.
The men from A-W
no X, Y or Z.

The photo

It was us,
over twenty years ago.
We were in our late 20's then.
This was a rare thing to see,
both of us together,
laughing,
and smiling.
We were always at odds.
 Our arms were around one another.
 This photo was during Christmas time.
 I only know because of the headband I am wearing.
 You cooked a feast for the guests that day.
Anyone who saw this photo,
would see two happy people.
No one would know,
they secretly loved one another.
Both people afraid to express that love with the other.
Masking their feelings,
with jokes, laughter and a friendship.
 Recently, that photo was tossed away.
 It represented hope for a love that secretly grew.
 A love that was stored in a safe,
 just as the photo was.
 An affection that did not happen.
 A wish that would never occur.
 A friendship that abruptly was placed on pause,
 even unknowingly almost ended.

A dream that one person was afraid to pursue,
for fear of rejection.
The photo is now missing.
It represented a time when two people,
Who hid behind a shell of their former selves.
After decades,
one who decided to take a chance
and profess his love.
The other,
threw caution to the wind
and embraced the man who loved her for years.

References

The keen memory of Brenda L. Alvarado (that's me).

Made in the USA
Middletown, DE
10 February 2021

32741321R00056